Collected Ghazals

Also by Jim Harrison

COLLECTED GHAZALS

JIM HARRISON

COPPER CANYON PRESS
PORT TOWNSEND, WASHINGTON

Gratitude, once again, to archivists, present and past, at Grand Valley State University, Annie Benefiel, Leigh Rupinski, and Nancy Richard.

Excerpts from reviews in the editor's note come from the following
publications: *The Hudson Review* (Winter 1971–72); *Library Journal* (June 1, 1971);
The New York Times Book Review (July 18 and December 5, 1971);
Survey of Contemporary Literature (1971); Rebecca Solnit, *The Mother of All
Questions* (Haymarket Books, 2017).

Copper Canyon Press is in residence at Fort Worden State Park
in Port Townsend, Washington, under the auspices of Centrum.
Centrum is a gathering place for artists and creative thinkers
from around the world, students of all ages and backgrounds,
and audiences seeking extraordinary cultural enrichment.

Library of Congress Cataloging-in-Publication Data

Names: Harrison, Jim, 1937–2016, author. | Bednarik, Joseph, 1964– editor.
Title: Collected ghazals / Jim Harrison ; [edited by Joseph Bednarik].
Description: Port Townsend : Copper Canyon Press, 2020. | Includes index. |
    Summary: "The collected ghazals of Jim Harrison"—Provided by publisher.
Identifiers: LCCN 2020017902 | ISBN 9781556595929 (paperback)
Subjects: LCSH: Ghazals, American.
Classification: LCC PS3558.A67 A6 2020 | DDC 811/.54—dc23
LC record available at https://lccn.loc.gov/2020017902

Copper Canyon Press
Post Office Box 271
Port Townsend, Washington 98368
www.coppercanyonpress.org

for Russell Chatham (1939–2019)

It is the lamp on the kitchen table
well after midnight saying nothing but light.

*The necessity of a necessity
finding its form.*
DAN GERBER

CONTENTS

Editor's Note

W HEN *Outlyer and Ghazals* appeared in 1971, Jim Harrison was living in rural northern Michigan, almost in poverty. He had recently vacated an academic position at Stony Brook University to make his living – *or not* – as a writer. Life inside an English department did not suit him, and as he recalls in the introduction to *The Shape of the Journey: New and Collected Poems,* he began writing ghazals while at Stony Brook "as a reaction to being terribly overstuffed with culture."

Outlyer and Ghazals was Harrison's third book – all poetry to that point – and at year's end was one of a handful of poetry titles included on the coveted *New York Times Book Review* "Noteworthy Titles" list. (The list that year also included poetry books by Adrienne Rich, Robert Hayden, and Octavio Paz.) The *Times* review prompting the honor was written by literary critic and *The Nation* poetry editor M.L. Rosenthal, and concluded:

> With each ghazal and in the ebb and flow and shifting emphasis of the clusters within the entire sequence, all the poetic faces and voices of Jim Harrison make themselves felt. It is sometimes exasperating, sometimes cheaply facile, often heartbreaking, often exquisitely beautiful as the

waves of language and sense-impressions and uncontrollably black moods and randy philosophizing and esthetic balancings sweep over the pages. This is poetry worth loving, hating, and fighting over, a subjective mirror of our American days and needs.

To be sure, by the time this laudatory review appeared, the "loving, hating, and fighting over" the ghazals were well underway. *Library Journal* was brutal in its assessment: "This volume is probably of little interest to anyone who enjoys reading poetry." The *Hudson Review* bit even harder, quoting one of Harrison's couplets:

I want to die in the saddle. An enemy of civilization
I want to walk around in the woods, fish and drink.

The reviewer then asking, "Who's stopping him?"

Turns out, nobody stopped him. For the rest of his life, Jim Harrison kept walking in the woods, kept fishing and drinking, and as nearly forty books in multiple genres attest, kept writing.

As for his becoming an "enemy of civilization," some readers and critics granted Jim Harrison his wish, no doubt using certain and specific couplets within the ghazals to make their case. What the *New York Times Book Review* called "uncontrollably black moods and randy philosophizing" was also called out as misogynist and violent. "These poems are direct and open, like a shotgun blast to the face. The analogy is not an exaggeration," wrote the *Survey of Contemporary Literature*. "The history of man's self-destruction is treated by the poet with the glibness of emotional violence: 'If you laid out all the limbs from the Civil War hospital / in Washington they would encircle the White House seven times.'"

And it is notable that as Harrison's writing career expanded to other genres, his name appeared on provocative lists and in critical essays, such as "10 Misogynistic Novels Every Woman Should Read" and "80 Books No Woman Should Read," though in the latter, Rebecca Solnit writes, "I forgave Kerouac eventually, just as I forgave Jim Harrison his objectifying lecherousness on the page, because they have redeeming qualities."

With *Collected Ghazals,* readers can experience the entirety of the published ghazals and decide for themselves. As Jim Harrison wrote in the essay "First Person Female," about his writing fiction in the voice of a woman, "The answer is always in the entire story, not a piece of it."

In preparation for this book, I visited the exhaustive Jim Harrison literary archive at Grand Valley State University. Within that archive, in its own acid-free folder, is an undated handwritten postcard from Adrienne Rich – the poet credited with bringing ghazals to broader awareness in the United States – which reads in part:

> Dear Jim,
> I really want to see those ghazals – please do send. . . .
> The idea that you've written them moves me very much.
> Love, Adrienne.

Holding that postcard in the library quiet, I could easily imagine Jim Harrison finding it inside his rural-route mailbox – along with a dentist bill he couldn't pay – and reading Rich's invitation more than

once, then slipping the treasure into his coat pocket and heading off
to walk around in the woods, fish, and drink.

Joseph Bednarik
Port Townsend, Washington

Collected Ghazals

NOTES ON THE GHAZALS

POEMS ARE ALWAYS better than a bloody turkey foot in the mailbox. Few would disagree. Robert Creeley once said, partly reconstituting Olson, "Form is never more than an extension of content." True and sage. We choose what suits us and will not fairly wear what doesn't fit. Don't try to bury a horse in a human coffin, no matter how much you loved the horse, or stick some mute, lovely butterfly or luna moth in a damp cavern. I hate to use the word, but form must be an "organic" revelation of content or the poem, however otherwise lively, will strike us false or merely tricky, an exercise in wit, crochet, pale embroidery.

The ghazal is an antique form dating from the thirteenth century and practiced by hundreds of poets since in languages as varied as Urdu, Arabic, Pashto, Turkish, Persian, German, French, and Spanish. Even Goethe and Schlegel wrote ghazals. Among my own contemporaries, Adrienne Rich has been especially successful with the form. I have not adhered to the strictness of metrics and structure of the ancient practitioners, with the exception of using a minimum of five couplets. The couplets are not related by reason or logic and their only continuity is made by a metaphorical jump. Ghazals are essentially lyrics and I have worked with whatever aspect of our life now that seemed to want to enter my field of vision. Crude, holy, natural, political, sexual. After several years spent with longer forms

I've tried to regain some of the spontaneity of the dance, the song unencumbered by any philosophical apparatus, faithful only to its own music.

J.H.

DRINKING SONG

I want to die in the saddle. An enemy of civilization
I want to walk around in the woods, fish and drink.

I'm going to be a child about it and I can't help it, I was
born this way and it makes me very happy to fish and drink.

I left when it was still dark and walked on the path to the
river, the Yellow Dog, where I spent the day fishing and drinking.

After she left me and I quit my job and wept for a year and
all my poems were born dead, I decided I would only fish and drink.

Water will never leave earth and whiskey is good for the brain.
What else am I supposed to do in these last days but fish and drink?

In the river was a trout, and I was on the bank, my heart in my
chest, clouds above, she was in NY forever and I, fishing and drinking.

Ghazals

I

Unbind my hair, she says. The night is white and warm,
the snow on the mountains absorbing the moon.

We have to get there before the music begins, scattered,
elliptical, needing to be drawn together and sung.

They have dark green voices and listening, there are birds,
coal shovels, the glazed hysteria of the soon-to-be-dead.

I suspect Jesus *will* return and the surprise will be
fatal. I'll ride the equator on a whale, a giraffe on land.

Even stone when inscribed bears the ecstatic. Pressed to
some new wall, ungiving, the screams become thinner.

Let us have the tambourine and guitars and forests, fruit,
and a new sun to guide us, a holy book, tracked in new blood.

II

I load my own shells and have a suitcase of pressed
cardboard. Naturally I'm poor and picturesque.

My father is dead and doesn't care if his vault leaks,
that his casket is cheap, his son a poet and a liar.

All the honest farmers in my family's past are watching
me through the barn slats, from the corncrib and hogpen.

Ghosts demand more than wives & teachers. I'll make a
"V" of my two books and plow a furrow in the garden.

And I want to judge the poetry table at the County Fair.
A new form, poems stacked in pyramids like prize potatoes.

This county agent of poetry will tell poets, "More potash
& nitrogen, the rows are crooked and the field limp, depleted."

III

The alfalfa was sweet and damp in fields where shepherds
lay once and rams strutted and Indians left signs of war.

He harnesses the horses drawing the wagon of wheat toward
the road, ground froze, an inch of sifting snow around their feet.

She forks the hay into the mow, in winter is a hired girl
in town and is always tired when she gets up for school.

Asleep again between peach rows, drunk at midmorning and something
conclusive is needed, a tooth pulled, a fistfight, a girl.

Would any god come down from where and end a small war between
two walls of bone, brain veering, bucking in fatal velocity?

IV

Near a brown river with carp no doubt pressing their
round pursed mouths to the river's bed. Tails upward.

Watching him behind his heifer, standing on a milk
stool, flies buzzing and sister cows swishing tails.

In the tree house the separate nickels placed in her hand.
Skirt rises, her dog yelps below and can't climb ladders.

River and barn and tree. Field where wheat is scarcely high
enough to hide, in light rain knees on pebbles and March mud.

In the brain with Elinor and Sonia, Deirdre of course
in dull flare of peat and Magdalen fresh from the troops.

I want to be old, and old, young. With these few bodies at
my side in a creel with fresh ferns & flowers over them.

V

Yes yes yes it was the year of the tall ships
and the sea owned more and larger fish.

Antiquarians know that London's gutters were
pissed into openly and daggers worn by whores.

Smart's Jeoffry had distant relatives roaming
the docks hungry for garbage at dawn. Any garbage.

O Keats in Grasmere, walking, walking. Tom
is dead and this lover is loverless, loving.

Wordsworth stoops, laughs only once a month and then
in private, mourns a daughter on another shore.

But Keats's heart, Keats in Italy, Keats's heart
Keats how I love thee, I love thee John Keats.

VI

Now changed. None come to Carthage. No cauldrons, all love
comes without oily sacraments. Skin breathes cooler air.

And light was there and two cliff swallows hung and swooped
for flies, audible heat from the field where steers fed.

I'm going to Stonehenge to recant, or from the manure pile
behind this shed I'm going to admit to a cow that I've lied.

He writes with a putty knife and goo, at night the North Star
hangs on the mountain peak like a Christmas ornament.

On the table the frozen rattlesnake thaws, the perfect club!
The perfect crime! Soon now to be skinned for my hatband.

VII

Says he, "Ah Edward I too have a dark past of manual labor."
But now Trivium Charontis seem to want me for Mars.

If her thighs weigh 21 pounds apiece what do her lips weigh?
Do that trick where you touch your toes. Do that right now.

The bold U.S.A. cowpoke in Bozeman, Montana, hates hippies,
cuts off their hair, makes $200 a month, room and board.

We want the sow bear that killed Clark's sheep to go away.
She has two cubs but must die for her terrible appetite.

Girl-of-my-dreams if you'll be mine I'll give up poetry
and be your index finger, lapdog, donkey, obvious unicorn.

VIII

The color of a poppy and bruised, the subalpine green that
ascends the mountainside from where the eagle looked at sheep.

Her sappy brain fleers, is part of the satin shirt (Western) she
wears, chartreuse with red scarf. Poeet he says with two *ee*s!

The bull we frighten by waving our hats bellows, his pecker
lengthens touching the grass, he wheels, foam from the mouth.

How do we shoot those things that don't even know they're animals
grazing and stalking in the high meadow: puma elk grizzly deer.

When he pulled the trigger the deer bucked like a horse, spine
broken, grew pink in circles, became a lover kissing him goodnight.

IX

He said the grizzly sat eating the sheep and when the bullet
struck tore the sheep in two, fell over backward dead.

With her mouth warm or cold she remains a welcome mat, a hole
shot through it many years ago in Ohio. Hump. Hemp treaded.

Is there an acre left to be allotted to each man & beast so
they might regard each other on hands and knees behind fences?

The sun straight above was white and aluminum and the trout
on the river bottom watched his feet slip clumsily on the rocks.

I want an obscene epitaph, one that will disgust the Memorial
Day crowds so that they'll indignantly topple my gravestone.

X

Praise me at Durkheim Fair where I've never been, hurling
grenade wursts at those who killed my uncle back in 1944.

Nothing is forgiven. The hurt child is thirty-one years old
and the girl in the pale blue dress walks out with another.

Where love lies. In the crawl space under the back porch
thinking of the aunt seen shedding her black bathing suit.

That girl was rended by the rapist. I'll send her a healing
sonnet in heaven. Forgive us. Forgive us. Forgive us.

The moon I saw through her legs beneath the cherry tree had
no footprints on it and a thigh easily blocked out its light.

Lauren Hutton has replaced Norma Jean, Ava Gardner, Lee Remick
and Vanessa Redgrave in my Calvinist fantasies. Don't go away.

XI

The brain opens the hand which touches that spot, clinically
soft, a member raises from his chair and insists upon his rights.

In some eye bank a cornea is frozen in liquid nitrogen. One day
my love I'll see your body from the left side of my face.

Half the team, a Belgian mare, was huge though weak. She died
convulsively from the 80-volt prod, still harnessed to her mate.

Alvin C. shot the last wolf in the Judith Basin after a four-year
hunt, raising a new breed of hounds to help. Dressed out 90 lbs.

When it rains I want to go north into the taiga, and before I
freeze in arid cold watch the reindeer watch the northern lights.

XII

Says Borges in *Ficciones,* "I'm in hell. I'm dead," and the dark
is glandular and swells about my feet concealing the ground.

Let us love the sun, little children but it is around too
much to notice and has no visible phases to care about.

Two pounds of steak eaten in deference to a tequila hangover.
His sign is that of a pig, a thousand-pound Hampshire boar.

Some would say her face looked homely with that thing sticking
out of it as if to feed her. Not I, said Wynken, not I.

The child is fully clothed but sits in the puddle madly
slapping the warm water on which the sun ripples and churns.

XIII

The night is thin and watery; fish in the air
and moonglint off her necklace of human teeth.

Bring O bring back my Bonnie and I'll return yours
with interest and exhaustion. I'm stuck between those legs.

Dangers of drugs: out in the swamp's middle he's stoned
and a bear hound mammothly threatens. Dazed with fright.

Marcia I won't go to Paris – too free with your body –
it's mine it's mine it's mine not just everyone's.

Now in this natal month Christ must be in some distant
nebula. O come down right now and be with us.

In the hole he fell in, a well pit, yellow jackets stung
him to death. Within minutes death can come by bees.

XIV

That heartless finch, botulinal. An official wheeze passes through
the screen door into the night, the vision of her finally dead.

I've decided here in Chico, Montana, that Nixon isn't president
and that that nasty item, Agnew, is retired to a hamster farm.

And that those mountains hold no people but geologists
spying on each other, and beasts spying on the geologists.

Mule deer die from curiosity – what can that thing be
wandering around with a stick, forgotten from last year?

Some tourists confuse me for an actual cowboy, ecstasy in
deceit, no longer a poet but a bona fide paper buckaroo.

I offer a twenty-one-gun salute to the caress as the blackflies buzz
around me and the rotting elk hides. The true source of the stink.

XV

Why did this sheep die? The legs are thin, stomach hugely
bloated. The girl cries and kicks her legs on the sofa.

The new marvels of language don't come up from the depths
but from the transparent layer, the soiled skin of things.

In London for puissant literary reasons he sits with the other
lost ones at a Soho striptease show. An endless oyster bar.

We'll need miracles of art and reason to raise these years
which are tombstones carved out of soap by the world's senators.

We'll have to move out at dawn and the dew is only a military
metaphor for the generally felt hidden-behind-bushes sorrow.

XVI

It is an hour before dawn and even prophets sleep
on their beds of gravel. Dreams of fish & hemlines.

The scissors moves across the paper and through
the beard. It doesn't know enough or when to stop.

The bear tires of his bicycle but he's strapped on
with straps of silver and gold straps inlaid with scalps.

We are imperturbable as deer whose ancestors saw the last
man and passed on the sweet knowledge by shitting on graves.

Let us arrange to meet sometime in transit, we'll all take
the same train perhaps, Cendrars's Express or the defunct Wabash.

Her swoon was officially interminable with unconvincing
geometric convulsions, no doubt her civic theater experience.

XVII

O Atlanta, roseate dawn, the clodhoppers, hillbillies, rednecks,
drunken dreams of murdering blacks; the gin mills still.

Our fried chicken and Key lime pie and rickets. To drain all
your swamps and touch a match, Seminoles forbidden drink.

Save the dogs everywhere. In France by actual count, Count
Blah Blah shot 885 pheasants in one day, his personal record.

There was a story of a lost child who remained lost & starved
to death hiding in a hollow log from both animals and searchers.

Cuba is off there beyond the Tortugas, forever invisible; Isle
of Pines where Crane wept, collecting tons of starfish and eels.

Her love was committed to horses and poets weighing less than
150 lbs. I weigh 200 and was not allowed into her Blue Fuck Room.

XVIII

I told the dark-haired girl to come down out of the apple
tree and take her medicine. In a dream I told her so.

We're going to have to do something about the night. The tissue
won't restore itself in the dark. I feel safe only at noon.

Waking. Out by the shed, their home, the Chicano cherry pickers
sing hymns on a hot morning, three guitars and a concertina.

We don't need dime-store surrealists buying objects to write
about or all this up-against-the-wall nonsense in *Art News.*

Even in the wilderness, in Hell Roaring Creek Basin, in this
grizzly kingdom, I fear stepping into a hidden missile silo.

My friend has become crippled, back wrenched into an "S" like
my brain. We'll go to Judah to wait for the Apocalypse.

XIX

We were much saddened by Bill Knott's death.
When he reemerged as a hospital orderly we were encouraged.

Sad thoughts of different cuts of meat and how I own no
cattle and am not a rancher with a freezer full of prime beef.

A pure plump dove sits on the wire as if two wings emerged
from a russet pear, head tucked into the sleeping fruit.

Your new romance is full of nails hidden from the saw's teeth,
a board under which a coral snake waits for a child's hand.

I don't want to die in a foreign land and was only in one
once, England, where I felt near death in the Cotswolds.

The cattle walked in the shallow water and birds flew
behind them to feed on the disturbed insects.

XX

Some sort of rag of pure language, no dictums but a bell
sound over clear water, beginning day no. 245 of a good year.

The faces made out of leaves and hidden within them, faces
that don't want to be discovered or given names by anyone.

There was a virgin out walking the night during the plague when
the wolves entered Avila for carrion. The first took her neck.

The ninth month when everything is expected of me and nothing
can be told – September when I sit and watch the summer die.

She knelt while I looked out the car window at a mountain
(Emigrant Peak). We need girls and mountains frequently.

If I can clean up my brain, perhaps a stick of dynamite will
be needed, the Sibyl will return as an undiscovered lover.

XXI

He sings from the bottom of a well but she can hear him up
through the oat straw, toads, boards, three entwined snakes.

It quiets the cattle they say mythically as who alive has
tried it, their blank stares, cows digesting song. Rumen.

Her long hissing glides at the roller-skating rink, skates
to calves to thighs to ass in blue satin and organ music.

How could you be sane if 250,000 came to the Isle of Wight
to hear your songs near the sea and they looked like an ocean?

Darling companion. We'll listen until it threatens and walls
fall to trumpet sounds or not and this true drug lifts us up.

That noise that came to us out in the dark, grizzly, leviathan,
drags the dead horse away to hollow swelling growls.

XXII

Maps. Maps. Maps. Venezuela, Keewanaw, Iceland open up
unfolding and when I get to them they'll look like maps.

New pilgrims everywhere won't visit tombs, need living
monuments to live again. But there are only tombs to visit.

They left her in the rain tied to the water with cobwebs,
stars stuck like burrs to her hair. I found her by her wailing.

It's obvious I'll never go to Petersburg and Akhmadulina
has married another in scorn of my worship of her picture.

You're not fooling yourself – if you weren't a coward you'd be
another target in Chicago, tremulous bull's-eye for hog fever.

XXIII

I imagined her dead, killed by some local maniac who
crept upon the house with snowmobile at low throttle.

Alcohol that lets me play out hates and loves and fights;
in each bottle is a woman, the betrayer and the slain.

I insist on a one-to-one relationship with nature.
If Thursday I'm a frog it will have to be my business.

You are well. You grow taller. Friends think I've bought you
stilts but it is I shrinking, up past my knees in marl.

She said take out the garbage. I trot through a field with the
sack in my teeth. At the dump I pause to snarl at a rat.

XXIV

This amber light floating strangely upward in the woods – nearly
dark now with a warlock hooting through the tips of trees.

If I were to be murdered here as an Enemy of the State you would
have to bury me under that woodpile for want of a shovel.

She was near the window and beyond her breasts I could see
the burdock, nettles, goldenrod in a field beyond the orchard.

We'll have to abandon this place and live out of the car again.
You'll nurse the baby while we're stuck in the snow out of gas.

The ice had entered the wood. It was twenty below and the beech
easy to split. I lived in a lean-to covered with deerskins.

I have been emptied of poison and returned home dried
out with a dirty bill of health and screaming for new wine.

XXV

O happy day! Said *overpowered,* had by it all and transfixed
and unforgetting other times that refused to swirl and flow.

The calendar above my head made of unnatural numbers, day
lasted five days and I expect a splendid year's worth of dawn.

Rain pumps. Juliet in her tower and Gaspara Stampa again and
that girl lolling in the hammock with a fruit smell about her.

Under tag alder, beneath the ferns, crawling to know animals
for hours, how it looks to them down in this lightless place.

The girl out in the snows in the Laurentians saves her money
for Montreal and I am to meet her in a few years by "accident."

Magdalen comes in a waking dream and refuses to cover me,
crying out for ice, release from time, for a cool spring.

XXVI

What will I do with seven billion cubic feet of clouds
in my head? I want to be wise and dispense it for quarters.

All these push-ups are making me a muscular fatman. Love would
make me lean and burning. Love. Sorry the elevator's full.

She was zeroed in on by creeps and forgot my meaningful glances
from the door. But then I'm walleyed and wear used capes.

She was built entirely of makeup, greasepaint all the way through
like a billiard ball is a billiard ball beneath its hard skin.

We'll have to leave this place in favor of where the sun
is cold when seen at all, bones rust, it rains all day.

The cat is mine and so is the dog. You take the orchard,
house and car and parents. I'm going to Greenland at dawn.

XXVII

I want a sign, a heraldic bird, or even an angel at midnight
or a plane ticket to Alexandria, a room full of good dreams.

This won't do; farmlife with chickens clucking in the barnyard,
lambs, cows, vicious horses kicking when I bite their necks.

The woman carved of ice was commissioned by certain unknown
parties and lasted into a March thaw, tits turning to water.

Phone call. That strange cowboy who pinned a button to the boy's
fly near the jukebox – well last night he shot his mom.

Arrested, taken in as it were for having a purple fundament,
a brain full of grotesqueries, a mouth exploding with red lies.

Hops a plane to NYC riding on the wing through a thunderstorm,
a parade, a suite at the Plaza, a new silver-plated revolver.

XXVIII

In the hotel room (far above the city) I said I bet you
can't crawl around the room like a dog hoho. But she could!

All our cities are lewd and slippery, most of all San Francisco
where people fuck in the fog wearing coarse wool.

And in Los Angeles the dry heat makes women burn so that
lubricants are fired in large doses from machine guns.

We'll settle the city question by walking deeply into forests
and in reasonably vestal groves eat animal meat and love.

I'm afraid nothing can be helped and all letters must be
returned unopened. Poetry must die so poems will live again.

Mines: there were no cities of golden-haired women down there
but rats, raccoon bones, snake skeletons and dark. Black dark.

XXIX

For my horse, Brotherinlaw, who had no character
breaking into panic at first grizzly scent.

Stuff this up your ass New York City you hissing
clip joint and plaster-mouthed child killer.

In Washington they eat bean soup and there's
bean soup on the streets and in the mouths of monuments.

The bull in the grove of lodgepole pines, a champion
broke his prick against a cow and is now worthless.

For that woman whose mouth has paper burns
a fresh trout, salt, honey, and healing music.

XXX

I am walked on a leash by my dog and am water
only to be crossed by a bridge. Dog and bridge.

An ear not owned by a face, an egg without a yolk
and my mother without a rooster. Not to have been.

London has no bees and it is bee time. No hounds
in the orchard, no small craft warnings or sailing ships.

In how many poems through how many innocent branches
has the moon peeked without being round.

This song is for New York City who peeled me like
an apple, the fat off the lamb, raw and coreless.

XXXI

I couldn't walk across that bridge in Hannibal
at night. I was carried in a Nash Ambassador.

On Gough Street the cars went overhead. I counted
two thousand or more one night before I slept.

She hit him in the face with her high-heeled shoe
as he scrambled around the floor getting away.

What am I going to do about the mist and the canning
factory in San Jose where I loaded green beans all night?

Billions of green beans in the Hanging Gardens off Green
Street falling softly on our heads, the dread dope again.

XXXII

All those girls dead in the war from misplaced or aimed
bombs, or victims of the conquerors, some eventually happy.

My friends, he said after midnight, you all live badly.
Dog's teeth grew longer and wife in bed became a lizard.

Goddamn the dark and its shrill violet hysteria.
I want to be finally sane and bow to all sentient creatures.

I'll name all the things I know new and old any you may
select from the list and remember the list but forget me.

It was cold and windy and the moon blew white fish across
the surface where phosphorescent tarpon swam below.

Ice in the air and the man just around the corner has a gun
and that nurse threw a tumor at you from the hospital window.

XXXIII

That her left foot is smaller if only slightly
than her right and when bare cloven down to the arch.

Lovers when they are up and down and think they are whirling
look like a pink tractor tire from the ceiling.

Drag the wooden girl to the fire but don't throw
her in as would the Great Diana of Asia.

Oh the price, the price price. Oh the toll, the toll toll.
Oh the cost, the cost cost. Of her he thought.

To dogs and fire, Bengal tiger, gorilla, Miura bull
throw those who hate thee, let my love be perfect.

I will lift her up out of Montana where her hoof
bruised my thigh. I planted apple trees all day.

XXXIV

When she walked on her hands and knees in the Arab
chamber the fly rod, flies, the river became extinct.

When I fall out of the sky upon you again I'll
feather at the last moment and come in feet first.

There are rotted apples in the clover beneath the fog
and mice invisibly beneath the apples eat them.

There is not enough music. The modal chord I carried
around for weeks is lost for want of an instrument.

In the eye of the turtle and the goldfish and the dog
I see myself upside down clawing the floor.

XXXV

When she dried herself on the dock a drop of water
followed gravity to her secret place with its time lock.

I've been sacrificed to, given up for, had flowers
left on my pillow by unknown hands. The last is a lie.

How could she cheat on me with that African? Let's refer
back to the lore of the locker room & shabby albino secrets.

O the shame of another's wife especially a friend's.
Even a peek is criminal. That greener grass is brown.

Your love for me lasted no longer than my savings for Yurp.
I couldn't bear all those photos of McQueen on your dresser.

Love strikes me any time. The druggist's daughter, the 4-H
girl riding her blue-ribbon horse at canter at the fair.

XXXVI

A scenario: I'm the Star, Lauren, Faye, Ali, little stars,
we tour America in a '59 Dodge, they read my smoldering poems.

I climbed the chute and lowered myself onto the Brahma bull,
we jump the fence trampling crowds, ford rivers, are happy.

All fantasies of a life of love and laughter where I hold your
hand and watch suffering take the very first boat out of port.

The child lost his only quarter at the fair but under the grandstand
he finds a tunnel where all cowshit goes when it dies.

His epitaph: he could dive to the bottom or he paddled in black
water or bruised by flotsam he drowned in his own watery sign.

In the morning the sky was red as were his eyes and his brain
and he rolled over in the grass soaked with dew and said no.

XXXVII

Who could knock at this door left open, repeat
this after me and fold it over as an endless sheet.

I love or I am a pig which perhaps I should be,
a poisoned ham in the dining room of Congress.

Not to kill but to infect with mercy. You are known
finally by what magazines you read in whose toilet.

I'll never be a cocksman or even a butterfly. The one
because I am the other, and the other, the other one.

This is the one song sung loud though in code: I love.
A lunepig shot with fatal poison, butterfly, no one.

XXXVIII

Once and for all to hear, I'm not going to shoot anybody
for any revolution. I'm told it hurts terribly to be shot.

Think that there are miniature pools of whiskey in your flesh
and small deposits of drugs and nicotine encysted in fat.

Beautiful enchanted women (or girls). Would you take your
places by my side, or do you want to fuck up your lives elsewhere?

The veteran said it was "wall-to-wall death" as the men had
been eating lunch, the mortar had hit, the shack blown to pieces.

We'll pick the first violets and mushrooms together & loiter
idyllically in the woods. I'll grow goat feet & prance around.

Master, master, he says, where can I find a house & living
for my family, without blowing my whole life on nonsense?

XXXIX

If you laid out all the limbs from the Civil War hospital
in Washington they would encircle the White House seven times.

Alaska cost two cents per acre net and when Seward
slept lightly he talked to his wife about ice.

My heart is Grant's for his bottle a day and his
foul mouth, his wife that weighed over five hundred pounds.

A hundred years later Walt Whitman often still
walks the length of the Potomac and *on* the water.

A child now sees it as a place for funerals and bags
of components beneath the senators' heads.

XL

If you were less of a vowel or had a full stop in your
brain. A cat's toy, a mouse stuffed with cotton.

It seems we must reject the ovoid for the sphere,
the sphere for the box, the box for the eye of the needle.

And the world for the senate for the circus
for the war for a fair for a carnival. The hobbyhorse.

The attic for a drawer and the drawer for a shell.
The shell for the final arena of water.

That fish with teeth longer than its body is ours
and the giant squid who scars the whale with sucker marks.

XLI

Song for Nat King Cole and the dog who ate the baby
from the carriage as if the carriage were a bowl.

A leafy peace & wormless earth we want, no wires,
connections, struts or props, only guitars and flutes.

The song of a man with a dirty-minded wife – there is
smoke from her pit which is the pit of a peach.

I wrenched my back horribly chopping down a tree – quiff,
quim, queeritus, peter hoister, pray for torn backs.

The crickets are chirping tonight and an ant crosses
the sleeping body of a snake to get to the other side.

I love the inventions of men, the pea sheller, the cherry
picker, the hay baler, the gun and throne and grenade.

XLII

New music might, that sucks men down in howls
as sea, please us if trapped in the inner ear.

When rising I knew there was a cock in that dream
where it shouldn't have been I confess I confess.

Say there this elbow tips glass upward, heat rolls
down in burns, say hallow this life hid under liquid.

Late in the morning Jesus ate his second breakfast,
walked out at five years, drove his first nail into a tree.

Say the monkey's jaw torn open by howling, say after
the drowned man's discovered scowling under the harbor's ice.

XLIII

Ghazal in fear there might not be another
to talk into fine white ash after another blooms.

He dies from it over and over; Duncan has
his own earth to walk through. Let us borrow it.

Mary is Spanish and from her heart comes forth
a pietà of withered leather, all bawling bulls.

Stand in the wine of it, the clear cool gold
of this morning and let your lips open now.

The fish on the beach that the blackbirds eat
smell from here as dead men might after war.

XLIV

That's a dark trough we'd hide in. Said his
sleep without *frisson* in a meadow beyond Jupiter.

It is no baronet of earth to stretch to – flags
planted will be only flags where no wind is.

Hang me rather there or the prez's jowl on a stick
when we piss on the moon as a wolf does NNW of Kobuk.

I'll be south on the Bitterroot while you're up there
and when you land I'll fire a solitary shot at moonface.

I wish you ill's ills, a heavy thumb & slow hands
and may you strike hard enough to see nothing at all.

XLV

What in coils works with riddle's logic, Riemann's
time a cluster of grapes moved and moving, convolute?

As nothing is separate from Empire the signs change
and move, now drawn outward, not "about" but "in."

The stars were only stars. If I looked up then it was
to see my nose flaring on another's face.

Ouspensky says, from one corner the mind looking for
herself may go to another then another as I went.

And in literal void, dazzling dark, who takes
who where? We are happened upon and are found at home.

XLVI

O she buzzed in my ear "I love you" and I dug at
the tickle with a forefinger with which I *knew* her.

At the post office I was given the official FBI
Eldridge Cleaver poster – "Guess he ain't around here."

The escaping turkey vulture vomits his load of rotten
fawn for quick flight. The lesson is obvious & literary.

We are not going to rise again. Simple as that.
We are not going to rise again. Simple as that.

I say it from marrow depth I miss my tomcat gone now from
us three months. He was a fellow creature and I loved him.

XLVII

The clouds swirling low past the house and
beneath the treetops and upstairs windows, tin thunder.

On the hill you can see far out at sea a black ship
burying seven hundred yards of public grief.

The fish that swam this morning in the river swims
through the rain in the orchard over the tips of grass.

Spec. Forces Sgt. Clyde Smith says those fucking
VC won't come out in the open and fight. O.K. Corral.

This brain has an abscess which drinks whiskey
turning the blood white and milky and thin.

The white dog with three legs dug a deep
hole near the pear tree and hid herself.

XLVIII

Dog, the lightning frightened us, dark house and both of us
silvered by it. Now we'll have three months of wind and cold.

Safe. From miracles and clouds, cut off from you and your
earthly city, parades of rats, froth, and skull tympanums.

The breathing in the thicket behind the beech tree was a deer
that hadn't heard me, a doe. I had hoped for a pretty girl.

Flickers gathering, swallows already gone. I'm going south
to the Yucatán or Costa Rica and foment foment and fish.

In the Sudan grass waving, roots white cords, utterly hidden
and only the hounds could find me assuming someone would look.

The sun shines coldly. I aim my shotgun at a ship at sea
and say nothing. The dog barks at the ship and countless waves.

XLIX

After the "invitation" by the preacher she collapsed in the
aisle and swallowed her tongue. It came back out when pried.

No fire falls and the world is wet not to speak of gray and
heat resistant. This winter the snow will stay forever.

The dead cherry trees diseased with leaf rot were piled and
soaked with fuel oil, flames shooting upward into the rain.

Rouse your soul to frenzy said Pasternak. Icons built
of flesh with enough heat to save a life from water.

A new sign won't be given and the old ones you forgot won't
return again until the moment before you die, unneeded then.

Fuse is wet, match won't light it and nothing will. Heat comes
out of the center, radiates faintly and no paper will burn.

L

A boot called Botte Sauvage renders rattlers harmless but they
cost too much; the poet bitten to death for want of boots.

I'm told that black corduroy offers protection from moonburn
and that if you rub yourself with a skunk, women will stay away.

There is a hiding place among the relics of the fifties, poets
hiding in the trunks of Hudson Hornets off the Merritt Parkway.

They said she was in Rome with her husband, a sculptor, but
I'm not fooled. At the Excelsior I'll expose her as a whore.

Down in the canyon the survivors were wailing in the overturned
car but it was dark, the cliffs steep, so we drove on to the bar.

She wants affection but is dressed in aluminum siding and her
edges are jagged; when cold, the skin peels off the tongue at touch.

LI

Who could put anything together that would stay in one place
as remorseless as that cabin hidden in the maple grove.

In Nevada the whores are less clean and fresh than in
Montana, and do not grow more beautiful with use.

The car went only seventeen miles before the motor burned up
and I sat in the grass thinking I had been taken and was sad.

This toothache means my body is wearing out, new monkey glands
for ears in the future, dog teeth, a pink transplanted body.

She is growing old. Of course with the peach, apple, plum,
you can eat around the bruised parts but still the core is black.

Windermere and Derwent Water are exhausted with their own
charm and want everyone to go back to their snot-nosed slums.

LII

I was lucky enough to have invented a liquid heart
by drinking a full gallon of DNA stolen from a lab.

To discover eleven more dollars than you thought you
had and the wild freedom in the tavern that follows.

He's writing mood music for the dead again and ought to have
his ass kicked though it is bruised too much already by his sport.

Both serpent becoming dragon and the twelve moons lost
at sea, worshipped items, rifts no longer needed by us.

Hot Mickey Mouse jazz and the mice jigging up the path
to the beehive castle, all with the bleached faces of congressmen.

LIII

These corners that stick out and catch on things
and I don't fill my body's clothes.

Euclid, walking in switchbacks, kite's tip, always
either *up* or *down* or both, triangular tongue & cunt.

Backing up to the rose tree to perceive which of its
points touch where. I'll soon be rid of you.

There are no small people who hitch rides on snakes
or ancient people with signs. I am here now.

That I will be suicided by myself or that lids close over
and over simply because they once were open.

We'll ask you to leave this room and brick up the door
and all the doors in the hallway until you go outside.

LIV

Aieeee was said in a blip the size of an ostrich egg,
blood pressures to a faint, humming heart flutters.

I can't die in this theater – the movie, *Point Blank,*
god's cheap abuse of irony. But the picture is fading.

This dry and yellow heat where each chicken's
scratch uproots a cloud and hay bursts into flame.

The horse is enraged with flies and rolls over
in the red dirt until he is a giant liver.

From the mailman's undulant car and through the lilacs
the baseball game. The kitchen window is white with noon.

LV

The child crawls in widening circles, backs to the wall
as a dog would. The lights grow dim, his mother talks.

Swag: a hot night and the clouds running low were brains and I
above them with the moon saw down through a glass skull.

And O god I think I want to sleep within some tree
or on a warmer planet beneath a march of asteroids.

He saw the lady in the Empire dress raise it to sit bare
along the black tree branch where she sang a ditty of nature.

They are packing up in the lamplight, moving out again
for the West this time sure only of inevitable miracles.

No mail delights me as much as this – written with plum juice
on red paper and announcing the rebirth of three dead species.

LVI

God I am cold and want to go to sleep for a long time
and only wake up when the sun shines and dogs laugh.

I passed away in my sleep from general grief and a seven-
year hangover. Fat angels wrapped me in traditional mauve.

A local indian maiden of sixteen told the judge to go
fuck himself, got thirty days, died of appendicitis in jail.

I molded all the hashish to look like deer & rabbit turds
and spread them in the woods for rest stops when I walk.

Please consider the case closed. Otis Redding died in a
firestorm and we want to put him together again somehow.

LVII

I thought it was night but found out the windows were painted
black and a bluebird bigger than a child's head was singing.

When we get out of Nam the pilot said we'll go down to S.A.
and kick the shit outta those commie greasers. Of course.

In sleepwalking all year long I grew cataracts, white-haired,
flesh fattened, texture of mushrooms, whistled notes at moon.

After seven hours of television and a quart of vodka he wept
over the National Anthem. O America Carcinoma the eagle dead.

Celebrate her with psalms and new songs – she'll be fifteen
tomorrow, a classic beauty who won't trouble her mind with poems.

I wanted to drag a few words out of silence then sleep and none
were what I truly wanted. So much silence and so many words.

LVIII

These losses are final – you walked out of the grape arbor
and are never to be seen again and you aren't aware of it.

I set off after the grail seven years ago but like a spiral
from above these circles narrow, tighten into a single point.

Let's forgive her for her Chinese-checker brain and the pills
that charge it electrically. She's pulled the switch too often.

After the country dance in the yellow Buick Dynaflow with
leather seats we thought Ferlin Husky was singing to us.

A bottle of Corbys won you. A decade later on hearing
I was a poet you laughed. You are permanently coarsened.

Catherine near the lake is a tale I'm telling – a whiff
of lilac and a girl bleeds through her eyes like a pigeon.

LIX

On the fourteenth Sunday after Pentecost I rose early
and went fishing where I saw an osprey eat a bass in a tree.

We are not all guilty for anything. Let all stupefied
Calvinists take pleasure in sweet dirty pictures and gin.

As an active farmer I'm concerned. Apollinaire fertilizer
won't feed the pigs or chickens. Year of my seventh failure.

When we awoke the music was faint and a golden light came
through the window, one fly buzzed, she whispered another's name.

Let me announce I'm not against homosexuality. Now that the air
is clear on this issue you can talk freely Donny Darkeyes.

A home with a heated garage where dad can tinker with his
poetry on a workbench and mom glazes the steamed froth for lunch.

LX

She called from Sundance, Wyoming, and said the posse had
forced her into obscene acts in the motel. Bob was dead.

The horse kicked the man off his feet and the man rolled
screaming in the dirt. The red-haired girl watched it all.

I've proclaimed June Carter queen-of-song as she makes me
tremble, tears form, chills come. I go to the tavern and drink.

The father ran away and was found near a highway underpass
near Fallon, Nevada, where he looked for shelter from the rain.

My friend the poet is out there in the West being terrified,
he wants to come home and eat well in New York City.

Daddy is dead and late one night won't appear on the porch
in his hunting clothes as I've long wanted him to. He's dead.

LXI

Wondering what this new light is, before he died he walked
across the kitchen and said, "My stomach is very cold."

And this haze, yellowish, covers all this morning, meadow,
orchard, woods. Something bad is happening somewhere to her.

I was ashamed of her Appalachian vulgarity and vaguely askew
teeth, her bad grammar, her wanting to screw more often than I.

It was May wine and the night liquid with dark and fog when
we stopped the car and loved to the sound of frogs in the swamp.

I'm bringing to a stop all my befouled nostalgia about childhood.
My eye was gored out, there was a war and my nickname was *pig*.

There was an old house that smelled of kerosene and apples
and we hugged in a dark attic, not knowing how to continue.

LXII

He climbed the ladder looking over the wall at the party
given for poets by the Prince of China. Fun was had by all.

A certain gracelessness entered his walk and gestures. A tumor
the size of a chickpea grew into a pink balloon in his brain.

I won't die in Paris or Jerusalem as planned but by electrocution
when I climb up the windmill to unscrew the shorted yard lights.

Samadhi. When I slept in the woods I awoke before dawn
and drank brandy and listened to the birds until the moon disappeared.

When she married she turned from a beautiful girl into a
useless sow with mud on her breasts and choruses of oinks.

O the bard is sure he loves the moon. And the inanimate moon
loves him back with silences, and moonbeams made of chalk.

LXIII

O well, it was the night of the terrible jackhammer
and she put my exhausted pelt in the closet for a souvenir.

Baalim. Why can only one in seven be saved from them
and live again? They never come in fire but in perfect cold.

Sepulchral pussy. Annabel Lee of the snows – the night's
too long this time of year to sleep through. Dark edges.

All these songs may be sung to the kazoo and I am not
ashamed, add mongrel's bark, and the music of duck and pig.

Mab has returned as a giantess. She's out there bombs in
fist and false laurel, dressed antigreen in black metal.

From this vantage point I can only think of you in the
barnyard, one-tenth ounce panties and it's a good vision.

LXIV

That the housefly is guided in flight by a fly brain diminishes
me – there was a time when I didn't own such thoughts.

You admit then you wouldn't love me if I were a dog or rabbit,
was legless with truly bad skin. I have no defense. Same to you.

Poetry (that afternoon, of course) came flying through the
treetops, a shuddering pink bird, beshitting itself in flight.

When we were in love in 1956 I thought I would give up Keats
and be in the UAW and you would spend Friday's check wisely.

Hard rock, acid rock, goofballs, hash, haven't altered my love
for woodcock and grouse. It is the other way around, Mom.

I resigned. Walked down the steps. Got on the Greyhound bus
and went home only to find it wasn't what I remembered at all.

LXV

There was a peculiar faint light from low in the east
and a leaf skein that scattered it on the ground where I lay.

I fell into the hidden mine shaft in Keewanaw, emerging
in a year with teeth and eyes of burnished copper, black skin.

What will become of her, what will become of her now that
she's sold into slavery to an Air Force lieutenant?

I spent the night prophesying to the huge black rock
in the river around which the current boiled and slid.

We'll have to put a stop to this dying everywhere of young
men. It's not working out and they won't come back.

Those poems you wrote won't raise the dead or stir the
living or open the young girl's lips to jubilance.

Marriage Ghazal

for Peter & Beck

Hammering & drifting. Sea wrack. Cast upon & cast out.
Who's here but shore? Where we stop is where shore is.

I saw the light beyond mountains turned umber by morning.
I walked by memory as if I had no legs. Or head.

In a bed of reeds I found my body and entered it,
taking my life upon myself, the soul made comfortable.

So the body's a nest for the soul and we set out inland,
the figure of a walker who only recognized the sea and moon.

And coming to the first town the body became a chorus –
O my god this is a place or thing and I'll stay awhile.

The body met a human with fur and the moon mounted her head
in an arc when she sat & they built a boat together.

The Chatham Ghazal

It is the lamp on the kitchen table
well after midnight saying nothing but light.

Here are a list of ten million measurements.
You may keep them. Or throw them away.

A strange warm day when November has forgotten
to be November. Birds form shrill clouds.

Phototropiques. We emerge upward from liquid.
See the invisible husks we've left behind called memories.

The press wonders how we drink so much poison and stay
alive. The antidote is chance, mobility, sleeplessness.

They've killed another cow. With the mountain of guts
I also bury all of the skins of thirty-seven years.

Faithful to Their Own Music:
The Ghazals of Jim Harrison

by Denver Butson

Sometime in 1999, right before my debut book of poems went to press, I was lucky enough to have the first of many dinners with the Kashmiri poet Agha Shahid Ali, poetry's most vocal advocate of the ancient Arabic/Persian poetic form the ghazal. We met at the Chelsea home of my publisher, Michael Carroll, and his lover, Edmund White. Ed cooked, smiling beatifically as he dropped, with equal measure, erudite observations about Proust or Nabokov and precise gossipy tidbits about the sex lives of ancient and contemporary literary royalty. Michael wisecracked irreverently, and Shahid, as he was known to friends, blurted out little gems of poetry while flirting dramatically with my wife. We drank a lot of wine. Late in the evening, Shahid realized that the last train he could possibly catch that night was soon to leave Penn Station, and Rhonda and I volunteered, or rather Shahid volunteered us, to walk him there.

As we hunched ourselves into a tunnel of Eighth Avenue wind, Shahid took me to task for the shortcomings of my ghazals. "Many of them are beautiful," he said, "but, my darling, they are *wrong!*"

The look on my face must have revealed my shock – how, after all, could poems be wrong?

"Ah," he teased, "you are like a typical American in the kitchen cooking for anybody with brown skin from 'over there.' You think that turning a dish bright orange with too much curry powder is somehow making a curry." He paused, laughing. "Simply writing in couplets, no matter how unrelated, is not writing ghazals."

Despite his train's imminent departure, Shahid schooled me on the requirements of a ghazal. I only fully grasped those lessons later, unblurred by wine and that fierce city wind. Though complicated at first glance, the form is really quite simple:

> a rhyme (the qafia) followed by a refrain (the radif) at the end of each line of the first couplet (the matla) establishes a pattern that is repeated at the end of the second line of each subsequent couplet;

> these couplets (at least five), roughly the same in syllable count and meter, need not cohere in subject matter or narrative sequence (in fact, the couplets are purposely unrelated) and must not run one to the next but stand alone like individual stones in a necklace;

> originally written anonymously, the ghazal should have the poet's signature in the final couplet (the makhta).

Shahid insisted that any poem that does not follow these basic rules is not a ghazal, just as any poem not fourteen lines in iambic pentameter with a Petrarchan or Elizabethan rhyme scheme would not call itself a sonnet.[1]

1. For those interested in learning the formal requirements of ghazals, an excellent place to begin is Agha Shahid Ali's introduction to *Ravishing Disunities: Real Ghazals in English* (Wesleyan University Press, 2000).

As we said our goodbyes, Penn Station glared down at us, a failure of its own aesthetic lineage, unlovely and utilitarian, stripped of the grand, opulent beauty of train stations. Still stinging, I blurted out my last challenge: "But what about Jim Harrison's ghazals?"

Shahid kissed my wife goodbye with a "My love, please call me," and turned to me. "Ah!" he said, "it doesn't matter whether Jim Harrison's poems are ghazals or not – and they are not, whatever he chooses to call them – because they are simply beautiful poems, just as they are." And then he vanished into the crowd funneling into the station.

~

I wish Jim Harrison had been at dinner that night. He would have found a kindred spirit in Edmund White, whom he hailed as "one of our bravest writers." They could have shared extravagant recipes, recalled memorable Parisian meals, and reminisced about their unlikely mutual friend, Thomas McGuane. I'm sure they would have traded bawdy tales. At some point, perhaps over more wine and dessert, Harrison would have loved to hear Shahid's take on his so-called ghazals. He likely would not have argued. Or cared.

Right away, Harrison made it clear that he had no interest in creating traditional ghazals, at all. In his introduction to *Outlyer and Ghazals* (1971) he writes: "I have not adhered to the strictness of metrics and structure of the ancient practitioners, with the exception of using a minimum of five couplets." In other words: no metrical consistency, no pattern-establishing matla, no radifs, no qafias, no signature makhta final couplet. Harrison's couplets, however, in true ghazal spirit "are not related by reason or logic and their only continuity is made by a metaphorical jump." In his very introduction to a series of poems he has chosen to name after this ancient form, Harrison shrugs off the form itself, demonstrating disdain for such restriction in the first place. "We choose what suits us and will not fairly wear what doesn't fit." And then, "Don't try to bury a horse in a human coffin, no matter how much you loved the horse." In other words, Harrison found it impractical and wrong to confine himself to a form, when poetry – or horses – in all its wildness and beauty, cannot be contained.

So, why did he choose to call these poems *ghazals* and adhere to the limitation of couplets? Here the answer seems to be in the abstract energy spurred by these deliberately disjointed couplets – the "modernness" of this ancient form. He says, again in his introduction, "I've tried to regain some of the spontaneity of the dance, the song unencumbered by any philosophical apparatus, faithful only to its own music." It is interesting but oddly consistent that Harrison, in his only foray into form in his published poetry, sees the ghazal as leading to spontaneity and song, while he is throwing off the very encumbrances that make the form what it is. Was his attraction to the ghazal simply a nose-thumbing at the current poetic establishment that eschewed form, and then his eschewing of the rules of that form just another nose-thumbing? Or could it have been that the ghazal's defiance of narrative line and story served as an antidote to the heavily narrative, confessional bent of American poetry since the 1950s? Others among his contemporaries were drawn to these oddly disconnected couplets. Harrison knew about Adrienne Rich's ghazals and must have been aware that others, including W.S. Merwin and Galway Kinnell, were writing them as well. Perhaps Harrison was simply seduced by the form's exotic lineage? Or does the answer lie more simply in the fact that one of his literary heroes, Federico García Lorca, wrote *gacelas* (the form has been traced to seventh-century Arabia and was quite popular in eleventh- and thirteenth-century Muslim Spain), and that even García Lorca also pretty much ignored the rules.

Whatever Harrison's incentive to confine himself even to this slightest limitation of form, his poetry is invigorated, simultaneously tightened by restriction and loosened by insistence on nonlinearity. Couplets demand concision – you can fit only so many words into two lines. And that those couplets do not have to cohere allows Harrison to jump swiftly from one topic to another. After writing poems in long form and fully open forms in his first two books, Harrison's poetry is freed, not confined, by these restrictions. The couplets clash, rub, and spark against one another as he explores his favorite themes – from everyday concerns of making a living to his personal and mystical connections to other animals, from unrequited lust for the unattainable to soul-crushing sadness that poetry really achieves nothing at all.

The strength of these poems lies in what Ali saw as the spirit of the ghazal – the "cry of the gazelle when it is cornered in a hunt and knows it must die." Further, Ali (A.S.) quotes Ahmed Ali's explanation that the form's unrelated couplets allow for "all human activity and affairs from the trivial to the most serious." Harrison's ghazals, despite their formal disdain, capture this spirit and are, as Agha Shahid said ghazals must be, "not an occasion for angst" but "an occasion for genuine grief."

Harrison's cries of the gazelle display a full spectrum of his obsessions and appetites, "from the trivial to the most serious." Because he loved counting – Harrison kept count of the birds of his life, saying the number would not be revealed until after his death (he also counted cars he heard while falling asleep and "countless" other things) – I counted the number of times some of these themes or obsessions come up in the ghazals. Chief among his references:

sixty to romantic love/lust/sex,
twenty-eight to spiritual/sensual connections to other
    animals,
twenty-two call for unity/disunity/newness,
sixteen to other artists, usually poets or musicians,
fifteen direct mentions each of death/dying and drunkenness/
    gluttony,
eleven concern war/antiwar,
ten to seeing, usually with some mention of his one good
    or one blind eye,
nine each of natural mysticism and of poverty,
eight of the moon,
seven each of the futility of poetry and of poetry as a
    practical activity like farming,
five direct mentions of counting itself.

Those familiar with Harrison's poetry would recognize these themes. His poetry drives directly or veers into these places, but in the ghazals, the voyage is presented in an imagistic mise-en-scène in which no story is told as linear narrative but in the accumulation of disparate cries, whelps, regrets, observations, and images.

One couplet can be about the movie stars he desires – here Lauren Hutton, Faye Dunaway, and Ali MacGraw take a ride with him:

A scenario: I'm the Star, Lauren, Faye, Ali, little stars,
we tour America in a '59 Dodge, they read my smoldering
    poems.

Another a recurring nightmare that his father, who along with Har-
rison's sister died in a car accident when Harrison was a young man,
is not coming home:

Daddy is dead and late one night won't appear on the porch
in his hunting clothes as I've long wanted him to. He's dead.

And another a fantasy that poetry be as essential and meaningful as
a farmer's produce:

And I want to judge the poetry table at the County Fair.
A new form, poems stacked in pyramids like prize potatoes.

The net effect of such metaphorical jumps is a holistic tour of the
mundane and the magical, the practical and the contemplative, the
mystical and the lustful. One necklace stone might be a yearning for
a woman the poet will never love; another, a lament about how little
money he has or believes he will ever have; and another might cele-
brate the eleven dollars he finds in his pocket and the joyful drinking
that follows. Harrison's unfettered consciousness leaps from hopeful
to abysmal, from romantic to guttural, from spiritual to embodied.
To be fair, decades since their original publication, some of these
couplets may offend contemporary sensibilities or seem comically
dated. Unconcerned or unaware of such sensibilities, the voice of
these ghazals offers an emotional and intellectual self in kaleido-
scopic bits, crashing together and breaking apart, breathlessly free
of narrative line or argument. In a kind of Zen negative capability,

they allow all thoughts, fears, dreams, and unresolved desires to arise without their author needing to order them into sense or argument.

When asked at a reading what the poem he had just read meant, my teacher, the great and stubbornly unclassifiable poet Theodore Enslin, simply read the poem again. Harrison's ghazals are such poems: they say what they say and mean what they mean. And if you, as reader, experience these ghazals as you might Zen meditation or music – allowing the couplets to wash over you and refraining from trying to force them into a meaning as they drift through your brain – you can be caught unaware by the specific beauty of the individual and profoundly moved by the cumulative power of the collective. Even without narrative, you can share in the longing and lamenting, the celebrating and the eating, the trembling from fear of the unknown and terror of the known, the counting and the quaking from nostalgia.

I confess: even after many close readings over the decades, I still cannot say what a single one of Harrison's ghazals "means." I would be hard-pressed even to say what all of them collectively mean, other than what all of Harrison's poetry means to me – the overwhelmingly naked chronicle of an active brain and hungry spirit beating fists against our finite boundaries, with bravado and lamenting, fully celebrating and grieving directly his short life on this earthly, bodily plane, often with minimal filter and the heightened perception of a monk or hunter. Each time I read these poems, I find that new couplets resonate with me. Here are several that I loved on my latest reading:

Unbind my hair, she says. The night is white and warm,
the snow on the mountains absorbing the moon.

Ghosts demand more than wives & teachers. I'll make a
"V" of my two books and plow a furrow in the garden.

In some eye bank a cornea is frozen in liquid nitrogen. One day
my love I'll see your body from the left side of my face.

I'll never be a cocksman or even a butterfly. The one
because I am the other, and the other, the other one.

The crickets are chirping tonight and an ant crosses
the sleeping body of a snake to get to the other side.

And in literal void, dazzling dark, who takes
who where? We are happened upon and are found at home.

Those poems you wrote won't raise the dead or stir the
living or open the young girl's lips to jubilance.

These couplets, like stones plucked from a necklace, stopped me
in my tracks this time. Next time I read the poems, different ones
will likely make me gasp or sigh. There is much in this storehouse
of images and revelations, as in Harrison's poetry as a whole, to
return to.

In my own process of writing ghazals, I have further restricted
myself (a more confining coffin, perhaps) to the limitation of bor-
rowing or stealing a line, usually from poetry, to establish my matla.
In this practice, I have often turned to Harrison's poetry. Sometimes I
return to a ghazal or two to remind myself that poetry need not make
the connections for the reader. When I am open to it, the jazz-like
leaps are exhilarating, inspiring, and edifying. There is pleasure, to
be sure, in reading Harrison's ghazals and allowing ourselves, as we

often do with dance and music and visual art, to experience the work without the brain trying to force the poem to confess, to set up and answer some riddle, to tell a story with a beginning, middle, and end. They are not easy to sum up or to reckon with if you go into them looking only for answers.

～

Just a year and a half after that tipsy, freezing Manhattan walk, and sadly a year before an aggressive brain tumor made quick work of the end of his life, Agha Shahid Ali published *Ravishing Disunities: Real Ghazals in English*. In his justly famous introduction, Ali witnesses to the power of the ghazal as he schools English-language readers on the strict requirements of his beloved form. The collection, not surprisingly, does not include Jim Harrison's ghazals, though Ali does mention him at the outset:

> I do like many aspects of the so-called ghazals by many American poets (among the more vibrant examples, I would single out James Harrison, Adrienne Rich, Robert Mezey, and Galway Kinnell) and could make a case for their discarding of the form in the context of their immediate aesthetics and see in their ghazals a desire to question all kinds of authorities by getting away from linearity and that crippling insistence on "unity."

James Harrison's ghazals: they ignored the rules and, according to the gatekeeper, became "simply beautiful poems, just as they are," capturing the *spirit* though not the letter of the law. And now in this stand-alone volume, they are ours to witness again in all their messy, brave, honest, grieving, lustful, longing humanity. Startling in their jump-cutting contradictions, Harrison's unconfinable horses are majestic and defecating, stately and fornicating, wildly scattered and symmetrically trotting, kicking futilely at the gate one minute and bolting into stampede seconds later, braying madly at the sky and then gazing silently at the ground beneath their hooves, one disjunctive couplet to the next. They are still and picturesque, just before or just after erupting into blurry gallop.

Index of First Lines

Please note that numerals refer to page numbers, not the numbered ghazals.

I load my own shells and have a suitcase of pressed, 10

In the hotel room (far above the city) I said I bet you, 36

I thought it was night but found out the windows were painted, 65

It is an hour before dawn and even prophets sleep, 24

It is the lamp on the kitchen table, 75

I told the dark-haired girl to come down out of the apple, 26

I want a sign, a heraldic bird, or even an angel at midnight, 35

I want to die in the saddle. An enemy of civilization, 5

I was lucky enough to have invented a liquid heart, 60

Maps. Maps. Maps. Venezuela, Keewanaw, Iceland open up, 30

Near a brown river with carp no doubt pressing their, 12

New music might, that sucks men down in howls, 50

Now changed. None come to Carthage. No cauldrons, all love, 14

O Atlanta, roseate dawn, the clodhoppers, hillbillies, rednecks, 25

O happy day! Said *overpowered,* had by it all and transfixed, 33

Once and for all to hear, I'm not going to shoot anybody, 46

On the fourteenth Sunday after Pentecost I rose early, 67

O she buzzed in my ear "I love you" and I dug at, 54

O well, it was the night of the terrible jackhammer, 71

Praise me at Durkheim Fair where I've never been, hurling, 18

Says Borges in *Ficciones,* "I'm in hell. I'm dead," and the dark, 20

Says he, "Ah Edward I too have a dark past of manual labor," 15

She called from Sundance, Wyoming, and said the posse had, 68

Some sort of rag of pure language, no dictums but a bell, 28

Song for Nat King Cole and the dog who ate the baby, 49

That heartless finch, botulinal. An official wheeze passes through, 22

That her left foot is smaller if only slightly, 41

That's a dark trough we'd hide in. Said his, 52

That the housefly is guided in flight by a fly brain diminishes, 72

The alfalfa was sweet and damp in fields where shepherds, 11

The brain opens the hand which touches that spot, clinically, 19

The child crawls in widening circles, backs to the wall, 63

The clouds swirling low past the house and, 55

The color of a poppy and bruised, the subalpine green that, 16

The night is thin and watery; fish in the air, 21

There was a peculiar faint light from low in the east, 73

These corners that stick out and catch on things, 61

These losses are final – you walked out of the grape arbor, 66

This amber light floating strangely upward in the woods – nearly, 32

Unbind my hair, she says. The night is white and warm, 9

We were much saddened by Bill Knott's death, 27

What in coils works with riddle's logic, Riemann's, 53

What will I do with seven billion cubic feet of clouds, 34

When she dried herself on the dock a drop of water, 43

When she walked on her hands and knees in the Arab, 42

Who could knock at this door left open, repeat, 45

Who could put anything together that would stay in one place, 59

Why did this sheep die? The legs are thin, stomach hugely, 23

Wondering what this new light is, before he died he walked, 69

Yes yes yes it was the year of the tall ships, 13

About the Author

Over a fifty-year writing career, Jim Harrison (1937–2016) published nearly forty books of poetry, fiction, and nonfiction, all of which remain in print. His work has been translated into two dozen languages. Legendary as a gourmand, Harrison wrote popular food columns for several journals and magazines, notably *Brick* and *Esquire*. In 2007, he was elected to the Academy of American Arts and Letters, and his extensive literary archive is housed at Grand Valley State University. Regarding his subject matter for writing, he said in an interview, "I like grit, I like love and death, I'm tired of irony."

About the Contributor

DENVER BUTSON'S "drowning ghazals" first appeared in *triptych* (1999) and since in several journals as well as the anthology *Ravishing Disunities: Real Ghazals in English* (Wesleyan, 2000). He has published five books of poetry, and his poems have appeared in *The Yale Review, Ontario Review, Field,* and *Caliban.* Butson's collaborations with musicians, filmmakers, and other artists have been exhibited and performed in the United States and in Italy. He lives in Brooklyn, New York.

Poetry is vital to language and living. Since 1972, Copper Canyon Press has published extraordinary poetry from around the world to engage the imaginations and intellects of readers, writers, booksellers, librarians, teachers, students, and donors.

WE ARE GRATEFUL FOR THE MAJOR SUPPORT PROVIDED BY:

THE PAUL G. ALLEN
FAMILY FOUNDATION

CULTURE

Lannan

OFFICE OF ARTS & CULTURE
SEATTLE

WASHINGTON STATE
ARTS COMMISSION

TO LEARN MORE ABOUT UNDERWRITING
COPPER CANYON PRESS TITLES,
PLEASE CALL 360-385-4925 EXT. 103

WE ARE GRATEFUL FOR THE MAJOR SUPPORT PROVIDED BY:

Anonymous

Jill Baker and Jeffrey Bishop

Anne and Geoffrey Barker

Donna and Matthew Bellew

Will Blythe

John Branch

Diana Broze

John R. Cahill

The Beatrice R. and Joseph A. Coleman Foundation

The Currie Family Fund

Laurie and Oskar Eustis

Austin Evans

Saramel Evans

Mimi Gardner Gates

Linda Fay Gerrard

Gull Industries Inc. on behalf of William True

The Trust of Warren A. Gummow

Carolyn and Robert Hedin

Bruce Kahn

Phil Kovacevich and Eric Wechsler

Lakeside Industries Inc. on behalf of Jeanne Marie Lee

Maureen Lee and Mark Busto

Peter Lewis and Johnna Turiano

Ellie Mathews and Carl Youngmann as The North Press

Hank and Liesel Meijer

Jack Nicholson

Gregg Orr

Petunia Charitable Fund and adviser Elizabeth Hebert

Gay Phinny

Suzanne Rapp and Mark Hamilton

Adam and Lynn Rauch

Emily and Dan Raymond

Jill and Bill Ruckelshaus

Cynthia Sears

Kim and Jeff Seely

Joan F. Woods

Barbara and Charles Wright

Caleb Young as C. Young Creative

The dedicated interns and faithful volunteers of Copper Canyon Press

THE HEART'S WORK:
JIM HARRISON'S POETIC LEGACY

COPPER CANYON PRESS is the steward of Jim Harrison's poetic legacy, and after his death the Press launched The Heart's Work, a multiyear, multibook publishing project designed to secure and advance Jim Harrison's reputation as a poet. *Collected Ghazals* is the second book; the initial publication, *Jim Harrison: The Essential Poems,* was called "passionate and sharp" in a starred review in *Booklist.*

Copper Canyon extends deep gratitude to the following for their generous support of The Heart's Work:

Anonymous (3)

Porter Abbott

Kirby North Ancona

Colman Andrews

Joyce Harrington Bahle

Carol Bawden and Scott Craig

Joseph Bednarik and Liesl Slabaugh

Susan Bergholz and Bert Snyder

Will Blythe

Sally and Maurice Bolmer

Chuck Bowden

David Brewster and Mary Kay Sneeringer

Michael Butler

Elise M. Cannon

Irene and Mike Cotter

Susann Craig

Guy de la Valdene

Bob DeMott

The Chinese character for poetry is made up
of two parts: "word" and "temple."
It also serves as pressmark for
Copper Canyon Press.

This book is set in Adobe Garmond Pro.
Book design by Gopa & Ted2, Inc.
Printed on archival-quality paper.